Amusement Park Science

Activity Book

Michael Dutton

DOVER PUBLICATIONS, INC.
MINEOLA, NEW YORK

When you open up the pages of this entertaining and educational activity book, you will take a trip to an amusement park. Once you are there, you will solve mazes, do a crossword puzzle, and spot the differences between two seemingly-identical illustrations along with learning some of the basic principles of gravity and physics. And you can have even more fun by coloring in the pictures as you go along!

Copyright

Copyright © 2015 by Dover Publications, Inc.
All rights reserved.

Bibliographical Note

Amusement Park Science Activity Book is a new work, first published by Dover Publications, Inc., in 2015

International Standard Book Number
ISBN-13: 978-0-486-78035-1
ISBN-10: 0-486-78035-X

Manufactured in the United States by Courier Corporation
78035X01   2015
www.doverpublications.com

It's easy to think that a classroom is the only place where we learn about science. But did you know you can explore some of the principles of physics and gravity at an amusement park?

You have probably heard of gravity, but even if you haven't you experience it all the time. It's what keeps you on the ground. The famous physicist Sir Isaac Newton explained this and more through the Laws of Motion when – according to legend – he experienced gravity in the form of an apple landing on his head.

What made the apple fall? It was the force from the center of the earth pulling the apple (among other things) toward it. This is part of the First Law of Motion, or Law of **Inertia:**

Objects stay at rest unless acted upon by a force. They continue moving in one direction unless acted upon by another force.

Newton is demonstrating the Second and Third Laws of Motion. By throwing an apple, his arm acts as the force that accelerates the apple, before gravity takes over: What goes up must come down! Illustrating the Third Law of Motion: For every action there is an equal or opposite reaction. Putting apples in a press results in fresh squeezed apple juice!

Phew! That was a lot of science just now. You totally deserve a prize from this booth!

While you're here, can you help Mr. Newton find all 18 apples?

Let's find our way through the log ride to better understand inertia and the **First Law of Motion.** The log naturally sits still, but the gentle downward flow of water moves it along.

The log builds up speed as it makes its way down. This combination of speed and direction together is called **velocity.** The water at the bottom of the ride slows down the velocity, using **friction,** causing two opposing forces to meet. The result? Getting soaked!

How about drying off on a breezy Ferris wheel? Unlike the log ride, there are no opposing forces to collide with the motion of the wheel. But there is still a unique type of motion to experience as you move in a steady circle.

Seated in your booth, you experience **centripetal force,** which comes from the center of the wheel. Each booth wants to travel in a straight line, but being attached to the wheel bends the path into a circle.

Now imagine what it must feel like on board an object whose direction is being affected by forces coming from multiple places! This ship is being rocked by the up and down motion of the waves, as well as the central pull of the whirlpool.

Pendulum rides mix these two forces to create a similar experience. That's one reason they all tend to look like ships. Luckily, you can experience the thrill of the stormy seas without the fear of being shipwrecked!

AVAST

SEEING DOUBLE?

You might be feeling a little dizzy after that ride. That's because your body hasn't adjusted to being on solid ground yet. It still thinks it needs to keep up with all the forces that were moving it on the ride!

FIND ALL 18 DIFFERENCES!

This may look like the same scene as the last page, but there are actually a few things that are off. See if you can find all 18. That is, once your stomach settles.

Carousel rides are another example of how centripetal force works. Even though the ride moves horizontally instead of up and down, the same principles of motion are at work. There's still room for excitement on a carousel, though. How so?

14

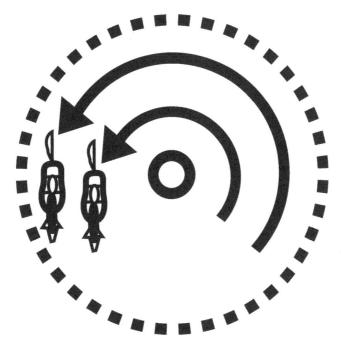

Well, did you know that if you ride on the horses on the outer side of the carousel it feels faster? That's because they cover one full rotation in the same amount of time as the horses on the inner side of the carousel. They have to move more quickly in order to cover more distance and still keep up.

And that's how **centripetal force** works. Is it any wonder we don't feel the same effect from our planet rotating around the sun? Luckily, we have these fun rides!

Now that you are experts on centripetal force, can you identify which
of these activities is using a different principle of motion?

If you guessed paddle ball, you're right. It uses opposing forces to create an action and reaction. What's the perfect ride to experience this effect? Bumper cars! But why are all the kids avoiding the big man?

Because when two forces act against each other, the bigger force absorbs less impact and the lighter person will always feel the greater jolt. Here are some other examples of opposing forces that just aren't fair!

Now that you know about Newton's third law of motion, it should be even easier to guess which things on the left should be used against the objects on the right.

But don't let these laws of motion discourage you from trying your hand at the High Striker attraction. With the right amount of force applied to just the right spot....

.... Who knows? You may hear that bell ring,
or knock down those stubborn metal bottles.

After all....

If there's one exception to science at amusement parks, it's that things aren't always what they seem! That's especially true in a funhouse, where silly mirrors bend reflections in funny ways.

We've hopped on several rides now, but it's time for the main event.
The star of the show. That's right. It's time for the roller coaster.

Roller coasters start off simple enough. A motor pulls you toward the top of the first hill. In much the same way you build up excitement (or pretend to be bored), the ride is building up **potential energy.** The stored energy is finally released once you top over the first hill.

FORCE

Direction + speed = VELOCITY

The first hill is always the highest so that maximum potential energy can become **kinetic energy** as you speed your way down. Build up enough speed, or **momentum,** velocity and centripetal force, and you can do loop to loops on some rides!

WHICH FORCE WORKS?

These three need a boost. Which of these would you use to get them going?

They've released kinetic energy but could use a change in direction to control their speed. Which option is the best?

How about now?

With so many ways to play with motion and force you can imagine that designing a ride must be just as fun as riding them.

t o o n i m

_ _ _ _ _ ◯ _

w o n e n t

◯◯ _ _ _ _

v a r i t y g

◯ _ _ _ _ _ _

n o t i c i r f

_ _ ◯ _ _ _ _ _

e p a l p

_ _ _ _ ◯ _

e c c e n s i

_ _ _ _ ◯◯ _

◯◯◯
◯◯◯◯◯

balloon, please.

Now that you've experienced the many ways motion and force can be played with, let's mix things up a little. Or unmix. Unscramble these words above, then use the circled letter in each word to spell out what the girl is saying.

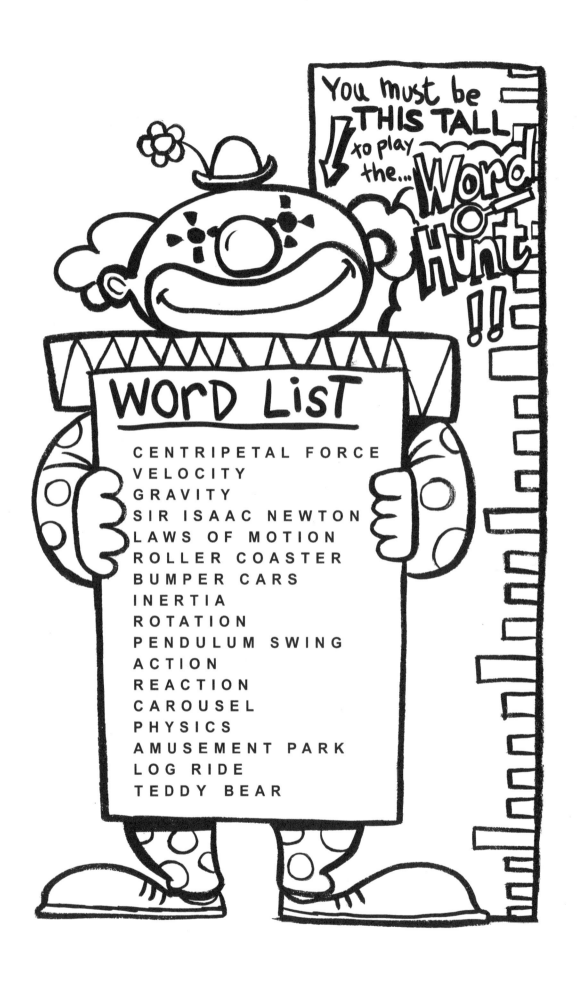

A	C	A	R	O	E	S	M	B	L	V	O	F	K	J	S	F	O	R
C	E	N	T	R	I	P	E	T	A	L	F	O	R	C	E	T	K	O
I	S	S	L	D	E	S	N	I	W	E	C	P	W	L	W	E	D	A
C	I	B	O	A	Y	V	K	O	S	S	J	F	K	J	S	D	R	T
S	R	R	O	L	L	E	R	C	O	A	S	T	E	R	J	D	E	C
T	I	S	G	K	E	S	P	H	F	P	I	N	E	R	T	I	A	K
I	S	T	R	A	E	T	J	L	M	H	L	O	G	R	M	S	C	B
L	A	S	A	F	Y	I	K	L	O	S	F	U	U	D	T	U	T	U
I	A	T	V	E	L	O	C	I	T	Y	P	F	M	K	E	M	I	M
L	C	T	I	W	O	N	M	P	I	Q	J	A	P	N	D	P	O	P
O	N	W	T	A	W	S	N	E	O	C	L	C	A	R	D	E	N	E
G	E	S	Y	K	G	A	M	T	N	N	A	T	K	J	Y	K	D	R
R	W	P	E	N	D	U	L	U	M	S	W	I	N	G	B	F	C	C
I	T	I	O	N	E	B	L	L	C	A	R	O	U	S	E	L	O	A
D	O	R	O	T	A	T	I	O	N	S	J	N	K	J	A	H	A	R
E	N	L	K	W	O	S	P	H	Y	S	I	C	S	H	R	F	S	S
G	R	A	T	I	A	M	U	S	E	M	E	N	T	P	A	R	K	F

Can you find all of the words on the list on the opposite page?
Be sure to look both up and down as well as across.

Let's take a train ride over to the Venn Diagram attraction.

COMPLETE THE...
VENN DIAGRAM

RIDES THAT MOVE...

...up and down

...round and round

example:

A Venn Diagram shows items sorted into categories drawn as circles. Things that have the characteristics of both circles are placed in the middle where the circles overlap. A ferris wheel, for example, is a ride that moves up and down **and** round and round. Can you sort the rest of these rides?

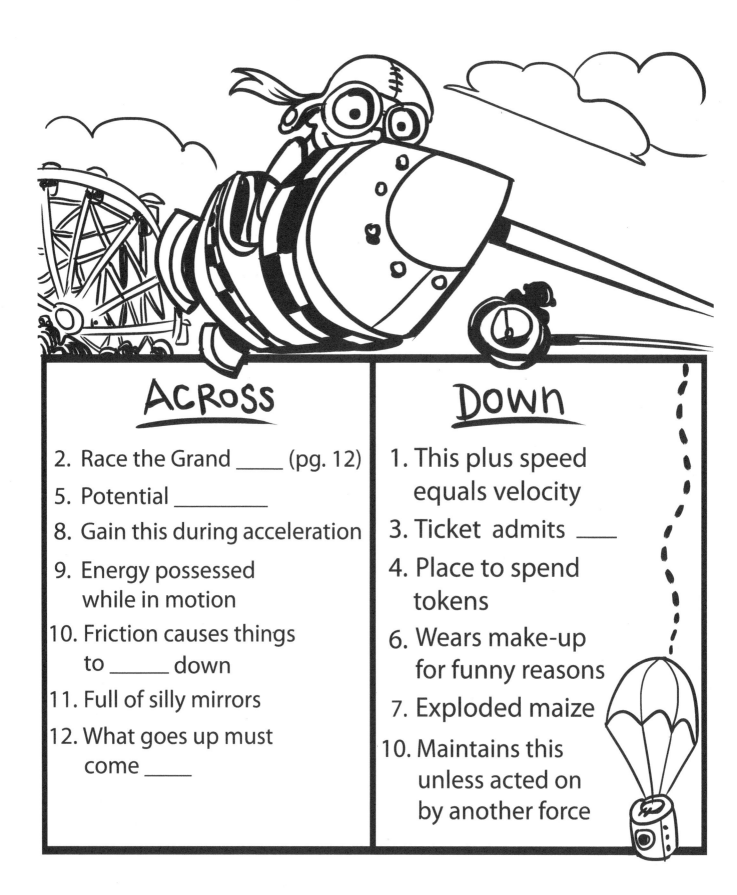

ACROSS

2. Race the Grand _____ (pg. 12)
5. Potential _____
8. Gain this during acceleration
9. Energy possessed while in motion
10. Friction causes things to _____ down
11. Full of silly mirrors
12. What goes up must come _____

DOWN

1. This plus speed equals velocity
3. Ticket admits _____
4. Place to spend tokens
6. Wears make-up for funny reasons
7. Exploded maize
10. Maintains this unless acted on by another force

Well, we've learned a lot today. Feeling pretty smart? Rocket scientist smart? Use the clues above to fill in the crossword puzzle on the next page!

That's it for this trip to the amusement park, but it's not too early to plan your next visit. Trace a path where every ride is visited one time without doubling back on your path. See you next time!

SOLUTIONS

page 5

page 6

FIND ALL 18 DIFFERENCES!

page 13

page 17

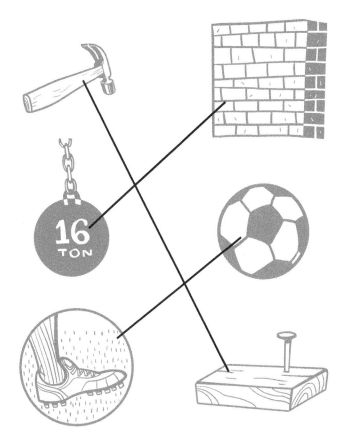

page 20

1. A motor moves the roller coaster.

2. A gradual turn to absorb speed.

3. All three are great ideas!

page 28

page 29

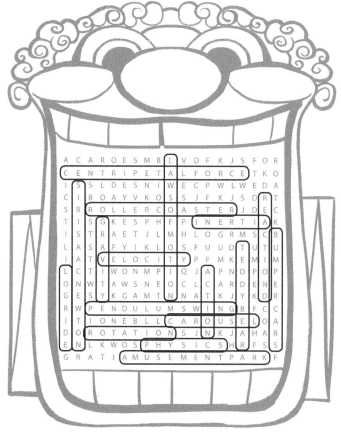

page 31

page 33

page 35

page 36